Rookie Read-About™ Science

Hearing Things

By Allan Fowler

Images supplied by VALAN Photos

Consultants:
Robert L. Hillerich, Ph.D., Bowling Green
State University, Bowling Green, Ohio

Mary Nalbandian, Director of Science,
Chicago Public Schools, Chicago, Illinois

Fay Robinson, Child Development Specialist

CHILDRENS PRESS®
CHICAGO

Series cover and interior design by Sara Shelton

Library of Congress Cataloging-in-Publication Data

Fowler, Allan.
   Hearing things / by Allan Fowler.
      p.   cm.—(Rookie read-about science)
   Summary: Discusses the sense of hearing and how it expands and
contributes to your world.
   ISBN 0-516-04909-7
   1. Hearing—Juvenile literature. [1. Hearing. 2. Senses and
sensation.] I. Title. II. Series.
QP462.2.F68 1991
151.1'5—dc20
                                                    90-22524
                                                       CIP
                                                       AC

    11 12 13 R 02

Your mother says,
"Good night. Sleep tight."

Maybe you aren't looking
at her when she speaks.
But you still can tell it's
your mother.

You know the sound of her
voice when you hear it.

Whenever you listen to people talk, or notice any kind of sound, you are using your sense of hearing.

Your sense of hearing tells you whether a sound is

loud, like a lion's roar,

or soft as a whisper.

Your sense of hearing tells you whether a sound is high...

like a whistle,

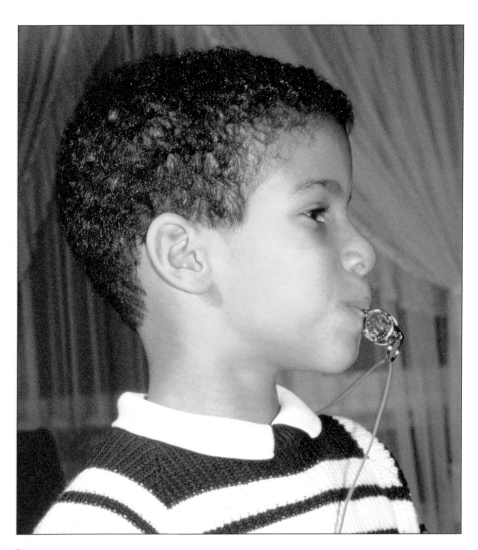

or low, like a tuba.

You hear with your ears.

This is what the inside of an ear looks like.

The parts of your ear work together to help you tell one sound from another.

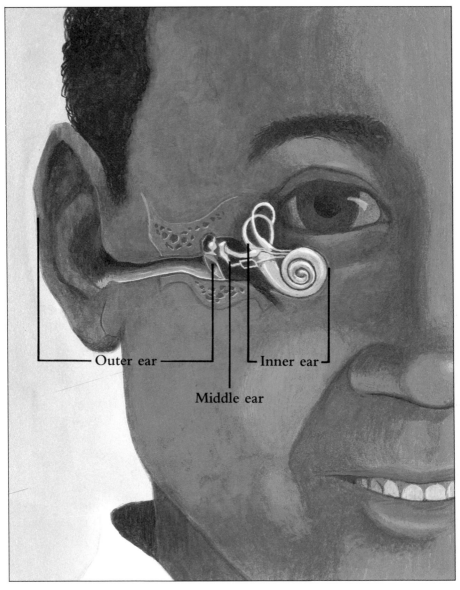

Outer ear — Inner ear

Middle ear

11

Do you know these sounds?

The clang, clang of a bell?

The whoo, whoo of an owl?

The whoosh of a waterfall?

The tinkling sound of a music box?

The happy clapping of an audience?

Do you know the sound
of your grandfather's laugh

and the cry of a baby?

Some sounds are so high
you can't hear them.
Dogs can hear them
because their ears are
different from human ears.

What sound is this wolf making?

What sound do you think this kitten is making?

Some sounds are very,
very loud, like jet engines
at airports.

People who work near jet
planes have to protect
their ears by wearing
special earmuffs.

Loud sounds can damage your ears. Even loud music from a stereo can damage your ears.

Sounds come into your ears
all the time, day or night.

Close your eyes for a minute and just listen.

What sounds can you hear?

Words You Know

sense of hearing

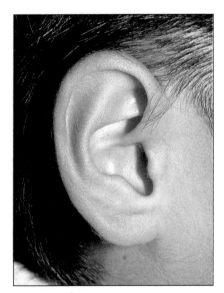

human ear

dog ear

loud sounds

soft sounds

special earmuffs

stereo

Index

About the Author

Allan Fowler is a free-lance writer with a
background in advertising. Born in New York, he
lives in Chicago now and enjoys traveling.

Photo Credits

Valan— © Johnny Johnson, Cover, 22; © Esther Schmidt, 5;
© Kennon Cooke, 6, 13, 26, 31 (Top right and bottom left);
© V. Wilkinson, 8, 9, 16, 17, 18, 21, 27, 28, 30 (2 photos), 31 (bottom
right); © James M. Richards, 14; © John Fowler, 15; © J. A.
Wilkinson, 19; © Dr. A. Farquhar, 24; © Aubrey Diem, 25, 31 (top left)

Illustration by Tom Dunnington, 11

COVER: Wolf